It Is In the Room
by Everkesia Taylor

It Is In the Room
Part One of The Elephant Series
By Everkesia Taylor

It Is In the Room
Copyright © 2019 by Everkesia Taylor

First printing, 2019

ISBN: 978-1-7322998-1-8

Cover Design by Anatasia Gorbunova
Edited by Susan Maphis

People are their truest selves when they are in the privacy of their own home... Now, imagine if there was someone or something watching them... Maybe the walls... Maybe an elephant.

Table of Contents

Table of Contents

It

Is

In

the

Room

She Is Out

She pours today from her pores,
Escapes; empties herself onto the floor
And sings out, "let the music rise,"
As she plays a game of tiptoe
Around the toxics of today.

It is time to unwind,
Get loose, redeem,
Cut clothes,
No more restraint,
No need to reserve.

She is out!

Out of mind,
Out of words,
Out of strength,
Out of power,
And it's okay.

In this room,
She needs none.
In this room,
She is out.

When I Think About It

I wonder what it would look like
If it stood right in front of me,
Full and bare as it is.

I wonder how it would feel
If it were to reach out and clasp
My face in its hand.

I wonder how it would taste
If its lips were pressed against mine.

I wonder how it would sound
If its voice were to whisper in my ear.

What would it say?

I wonder what I would do.

I Found Pride

Figments of my reality
Amalgamated with my dreams
As one truth,
One world.

Here were my human rights.
Inked on paper
Was the constitution that
Would emancipate me
From reality,

From being black,
From being a woman,
From being American,
Leaving me purely human.

There was a power.

It heaved my heart
With words,
And I liked the way
It felt to rise with pride
In my mind,

In my life,
In my story,
In the world I crafted
With my own
Bare, unholy hands,

And still, it was sacred to me.

Still, it was full of everything I needed,
Everything I've ever wanted it to be.

Undefined and Redefined

You cannot put it inside of a box,
You can't paint or draw it on a canvas,
It can't be held or kept,
It can't be summed or summoned,
It can't be stamped "approved" or "denied,"
It can't be picked or chosen,
It can't be pushed or grabbed,
It can't be said to be right or wrong.

You cannot put it inside of a box,
It can't be cooked or eaten,
It can't be burned or buried,
It can't be stomped on,
It can't be bent, cracked or broken,
It can't be hugged and kissed.

You cannot put it inside of a box,
It can't be shaped or carved,
It can't be created or colored,
It can't be seen or saved,
It can't be loved nor hated,
It can't be destroyed.

One can only describe
What it isn't,
Not what it is.
For, it is defined only
By its freedom.

There Are No Bounds

I can see white and black birds
Playing games in the sky,
I can see a woman applying lipstick
Using her reflection in the water,
I can hear the boys smiling as
The girls laugh at their broken attempts,
I can hear the serenading, seductive song of
The cruising ice cream truck, and see
The kids running into its trap,

All while sitting inside of a cage.

Yes, We Are Here. But, We Are Not Here

Come,
Let's forget about the
Walls we were born behind,
Of which we live within.

Come,
Let's imagine our lives
Outside of it, let's list
The possibilities that
Exist outside of this.

Wherever She Is

Wherever she is I hope there's water.
I hope the ground sings to the rhythm
Of her footsteps and I hope she dances to its song.

I hope there's water.
I hope the city is filled with smiles
And laughs, for she deserves to be
Enlightened by someone else's.

I hope there's water.
Enough to drink.
Enough to give.
Enough to waste.
Enough to swim.

I hope there's water.
I hope she walks with delight
As the flow of the world
Inspires her with poetry of its own.

I hope there's water.
I hope there are no
Walls where she is, but bridges
That leads across the largest body of water.

I hope there's clean water,
Pure water,
Genuine water,
Sterling water,
Aseptic water,
The perfect water for her.

I Know I Shouldn't, But I Do

I like how the arch
Of your eyebrows
Straightens and cringes
To the upper center of your forehead.

I like how your mouth
Shudders as your teeth bump.

I like how the pitch of your voice
Becomes thunder,

And how your eyes fall
From heaven to hell,
The same as your mood.

I know I shouldn't,
But I do.

Sorry I Left, But I Needed To Get Away

To a place where love couldn't
Reach out its hand and touch,
Scratch or pull me down.

To a place where the past
Never came to visit and the
Future was never invited,

A place where present slept
All day and celebrated all night long.

A place where freedom lived
With no cost to my sanity.

Sorry I left, but I couldn't
Find this there.

Sorry I Forgot

Maybe if it were
Written on my skin,
Or embedded in my bones,
Or smothered in my nose,
Or fused in my soles,
Or captured in my retina,
Or stuck in my teeth,
Or wrapped around my finger,
Or floating in my stomach,
Or hugging my spirit,
Or suffocating my soul,
Or tickling my toes,
Or curling the hairs on my arm,
Or making me scream for more,

Then maybe I could remember.

Everything and Nothing

She has something blue,
Something we've never seen before.

She has something white,
Something we all want.

She has something new,
Something we all need.

She has something green,
Something that grows.

She has something old,
Something her mother owned.

She has something near,
Something far from us.

She has so many things,
And to her it means nothing.

I Know Nothing

Everything that I am aware of
Lives within the dimensions
Of what is already here,
And I reach out and absorb it,
Some of it, most of it.

And it is enough for me now.

And it is all I know.
Nothing more.

Shadows Crawl

I like to watch it crawl
Across my skin,
Across the ground,
Across the water,
Across the mind,
Across my dreams
Of you and I together,
And across the time
That lives in between.

Crawling and
Crawling,
Until I,

Until I begin to crawl, too.

Depends On The Day

Yesterday,
I wanted to punch
You in the face,
Slap you,
Kick you,
Curse you,
And watch you burn.

Today,
I want to hug you,
Kiss you,
Feed you,
Love you,
And make you feel warm.

Even Though I Said, I Still Could...I Still Would

I want to grab you
By the shirt,
Pull you in close,
And whisper in
Your ear,
I miss you.
I'd whisper,
I love you.
I'd whisper,
I need you.
I'd whisper,
I want you.

And then I'd let you go.

Oh yeah, I'd let you go.
I'd even watch you leave.

The Maze of You

Moving forward
I turn,
Right.
Right.
Left.
Enter through the door.
You're not there.

Turning back,
I turn
Left,
Forward.
Forward.
Forward.
Quick right.
Now left.
Left.
Right.
I think I smell your scent.

Following forward.
Left.
Right.
Left.
Your scent is fading.

Left.
Right.
Left.
I think I am lost.

Outcome

Standing still in the chaos of silence
With wondering eyes,
Searching every inch
Of the room,
Trying to find you,

And I didn't,

And my mind began
To fill with doubt
As I got lost in the
Spotlight of crowds,

Again, where were you?

I Must Remind Myself

Nostalgia corrupts the present
By crafting a bridge
That I now have to
Set on fire.

Nostalgia is the reason
For my current
Heartbreak and
Disappointment.

I expect too much from you,
Not realizing that you are
A changed person,
And I am a changed person,

And today isn't yesterday.

For The Second Time This Week

Today,
I have fallen into the hole
Where the light of my dreams
Has detered into the darkness
Of my worst nightmare.

Again, today,
I am lost inside of the hole,
Rubbing my hands against
It's walls of nothingness,
Only to reveal to my mind
That I am nowhere, still…

The Wisdom of This Room

I didn't know
If I wanted to go,
Or where I would go, if I did.

So I stayed.
Listening to the walls
Tell stories of the people
Who once lived here.

The ones who loved,
The ones who were lost,
The ones who left,
The ones who stayed and died,
The ones who lived,
And never lived the lives
That was meant for them,
Or the versions they had
Dreamt of in this very room,
In this very bed.

And they said
I must be crazy
To stay, to listen to
The voice of a room.

But I knew that if I
Knew anything at all,
I knew the words were true
And I'd rather be crazy
Than a fool.

And plus, there was
Something I needed to hear.

I Am Not Claustrophobic,
But Damnit, I Am Claustrophobic

I cannot see it
To say,
But I can feel it
Inching closer to me
With its hand stretched out,
Reaching to GRAB ME,

And she is too far away
From me to help.

I am in need of help.

Because it is coming fast,
And I, alone, cannot stop it
From shrinking me whole,

And for the first time,
I am scared,
And unsettled
With words I've thought of
But could never say aloud.

Temporary Relief

When you laid your hand
On mine,
You took it,
The despair, the grief,
The sorrow, the void,
The emptiness, the loneliness,
The fear and the doubt...
All of it,
You took it.

And for the moment,
I was okay.

And when you let go,
I felt all of it drain back
Into me full force.

And I wasn't okay, again.

This Follows

I tried closing my eyes to escape,
But it seeped into my dreams.

I tried eating until my stomach filled,
But there was always room left for it.

I tried scrubbing it off my skin,
But the stench still followed.

I tried running it into the ground
With my bare feet, but it was
Fused in my soles.

I tried fighting it with my fist,
But it didn't fight me back,
So I could never win.

I tried ignoring it,
But its scream was so acidic
That it melted me in its pitch.

I tried killing myself,
But it wouldn't allow me to die.

I tried praying it away,
But it seemed out of God's reach,
Or maybe God wasn't listening,
Or maybe it is in God's plan.

I'd Rather Be Alone

I'd rather be here
Drowning alone,
Than with them
Drowning alone.

No one can convince me,
No one can heave me
From this without
My permission,
Without my help,
And I am too deep
In this water to
Help myself,
So, no!

I'd rather be here
Drowning alone,
Than with them
Drowning alone.

Because they'll regret it,
And I'll regret it too.

And I'll hate them for
Not knowing, for not
Being able to see me drown
As I stand right in front of them,

Coughing,
Gargling,
Shaking,
Panicking,

I'd rather be here
Drowning alone,
Than with them
Drowning alone.

Sorry I Haven't Called

Sorry I haven't called,

I've been stuck
In a room that is sable,
With too much space,
Too much air to breathe,

Too much time spent stuck.

I've been trying.
But the worships are quiet,
And I can't walk.

In my head, there's a way,
Down the stairs, up the road,
Turn left or right, choose neither,

I can only move forward,
I am trying, I promise.

But even when I figure it out,
It never lasts long enough to take me far.

I am still trying.

In my head,
I am in the middle
Of the road, lost,
Thinking about you,
Maybe I should call.

Junk Drawers

I feel like thread.
Looped, twisted, and tangled
With cords.

I feel like cords.
Lost, unwanted, unmatched,
And smothered by the thread.

I feel like pennies,
Dimes, and nickels.
Stuck beneath the cords and thread,
Plastered by the ketchup packets.

I feel like the ketchup packets.
Lost in a drawer with my insides seeping
Onto thread, cords, and coins.

I feel like the drawer.
Full of things.
Full of nothing.

I Know Them

If I were to say,
"I wanted to…"
Their initial response
Would be
"No, don't do that"
Instead of,
"Why do you feel that way?"

And right now, right now!
I need someone to say
"That's okay. You're okay."

I guess when the sun burns black
And the moon severs…

Hide and Seek

"Come out,
Come out,
Wherever you are."

She looks behind the door,
The window and shower curtains,
Underneath desk and bed,
In the closet, in cabinets,
Checks basement,
Checks attic.

"Come out,
Come out,
Wherever you are."

Silence.

(Maybe she isn't in the room.
Maybe she's not even in the house).

Wherever She's Going

I hope there's water.
I hope that every room she walks in
Is filled with warmth and light and tenderness
That touches her skin like soft fresh cotton.

I hope there's water.
I hope there's a place for her
To rest her mind from all the
Wonder and worry of her world.

I hope there's water.
I hope there's room for
Her to stretch, with every
Inch spreading free as air,
Fluid as water.

I hope there's water.
I hope all of her theories
Are tested, and questions are
Answered, in a manner that leaves
Her full and satisfied forever.

I hope there's water.
I hope she follows the water
And thinks about where she's been,
I hope she thinks of home.

She's a Little Different

The way she walk.
It's a little slower,
More gentle,
More careful than usual.

The tempo of her words.
It's a little slower,
More gentle,
More careful than usual.

Her smile.
It's a little wider,
More welcoming,
More free than usual.

Her eyes.
They're a little wider,
More welcoming,
More free than usual.

She's a little different,
Better than usual.

Follow @everkesia on Instagram for more information about upcoming books, EPs and events.

Q & A

What is the elephant poetry series about?

The series in its entirety talks about the things we are too afraid or too comfortable to talk about. It's about revealing the things that we consciously and unconsciously hide from others and from ourselves along with addressing the tension (the elephant) that is in the room. It explores the subjects of fear, love, dreams, depression, self-images, norms, police brutality along with many other battles that are faced on a daily basis.

Why an elephant and what does it represent?

The elephant is known for having a tremendous memory. And in terms of the book, it acts as a recorder. It holds the record of all of my struggles, fears, mistakes, challenges, actions, and so forth. Ultimately, the elephant represents the truth.

What does the series mean to you?

For me, it represents liberation and freedom. Writing this series has allowed me to empty myself from all I am filled with; from all of the things that somehow makes me feel trapped. And it's the freedom of being able to say how I feel, what I believe or what I want in such a way that holds no restrictions or boundaries; needing no one's permission or validation to do so.

23005131R00034

Made in the USA
San Bernardino, CA
18 January 2019